$\mathcal{T}$hat man alone acquires strength of
body and soul and attains to happiness whose
heart is free from doubt and is filled with truth.

Rig Veda, Sanskrit text, c. 1500 BC

*F*aith in ourselves

and faith in God –

that is the secret of greatness

for God is Love.

Sai Baba
Indian spiritual leader

*P*roof is the last thing looked for

by a truly religious mind,

which feels the imaginative fitness

of its faith.

George Santayana, 1863–1952
Spanish-born American philosopher, writer

*D*o not lose your inward peace

for anything in the world

even if your whole world

seems upset.

St. Francis de Sales, 1567–1622
French Roman Catholic bishop

$\mathcal{H}$ealth is the greatest gift,

contentment the greatest wealth,

faithfulness the best relationship.

Buddha, c. 560–480 BC
Indian spiritual leader, founder of Buddhism

I would not attack

the faith of a heathen

without being sure

I had a better one to put in its place.

Harriet Beecher Stowe, 1811–1896
American author, abolitionist, social critic

Quiet minds cannot be perplexed or frightened but go on in fortune or misfortune at their own private pace like a clock ticking during a thunderstorm.

Robert Louis Stevenson, 1850–1894
Scottish writer, poet, essayist

*N*or shall derision

prove powerful against those who listen to humanity

or those who follow in the footsteps of divinity

for they shall live forever.

Kahlil Gibran, 1883–1931
Lebanese poet, artist, mystic

*I*t is impossible that anything so natural,

so necessary, and so universal as death

should ever have been designed by providence

as an evil to mankind.

Jonathan Swift, 1667–1745
Irish satirist, poet, essayist, cleric

When a smart fit of sickness tells me this

scurvy tenement of my body will fall in a little time,

I am e'en as unconcerned as was that honest Hibernian,

who being in bed in the great storm some years ago

and told the house would tumble over his head,

made answer, 'What care I for the house?

I am only a lodger.'

Alexander Pope, 1688–1744
English poet

*N*ever think of God

but as an infinity of overflowing love

who wills nothing by the creation

but to be the comfort, the blessing,

and joy of every life according to its capacity.

And let this idea, which is the truth of truths,

animate and govern all that you think or say or do

either towards God or man.

William Law, 1686–1761
English spiritual writer

My faith has been the driving thing of my life.

I think it is important that people

who are perceived as liberals

not be afraid of talking about moral

and community values.

Marian Wright Edelman, b. 1939
American civil rights campaigner

The only way to meet affliction

is to pass through it solemnly, slowly,

with humility and faith,

as the Israelites passed through the sea.

Then its very waves of misery will divide

and become to us a wall

on the right side and on the left

until the gulf narrows before our eyes,

and we land safe on the opposite shore.

Dinah Maria Mulock, 1826–1887
British novelist

As one can ascend to the top of a house

by means of a ladder or a bamboo

or a staircase or a rope,

so diverse are the ways and means

to approach God,

and every religion in the world

shows one of these ways.

Sri Ramakrishna, 1836–1886
Indian spiritual leader

I love you, my brother,

whoever you are – whether you worship in your church,

kneel in your temple, or pray in your mosque.

You and I are all children of one faith.

Kahlil Gibran, 1882–1931
Lebanese poet, artist, mystic

If I were dying,

my last words would be,

'Have faith and pursue the unknown end.'

Oliver Wendell Holmes, Jr., 1841–1935
American jurist, judge

Charity enough to see some good in your neighbor.

Love enough to move you to be useful

and helpful to others.

Faith enough to make real the things of God.

Hope enough to remove all anxious fears

concerning the future.

Johann Wolfgang von Goethe, 1749–1832
German poet, writer, dramatist, scientist

*N*ine requisites for contented living:

Health enough to make work a pleasure.

Wealth enough to support your needs.

Strength to battle with difficulties and overcome them.

Grace enough to confess your sins and forsake them.

Patience enough to toil until some good is accomplished.

A lover never seeks

without being sought by his beloved.

When the lightning bolt of love has pierced the heart,

be assured that there is love in that heart.

When the love of God grows in your heart,

beyond any doubt God loves you.

Rumi, 1207–1273
Persian poet

A little more patience,

a little more charity for all,

a little more devotion, a little more love;

with less bowing down to the past,

and a silent ignoring of pretended authority;

brave looking forward to the future

with more faith in our fellows,

and the race will be ripe

for a great burst of light and life.

Elbert Hubbard, 1856–1915
American editor, writer, businessman

I always prefer to believe the best of everybody –

it saves so much trouble.

Rudyard Kipling, 1865–1936
Indian-born British poet, writer

$\mathcal{A}$lways continue the climb.

It is possible for you to do whatever you choose

if you first get to know who you are

and are willing to work with a power

that is greater than ourselves to do it.

Oprah Winfrey, b. 1954
American television personality

The sea does not reward those who are too anxious, too greedy, or too impatient. To dig for treasures shows not only impatience and greed but lack of faith. Patience, patience, patience is what the sea teaches. Patience and faith. One should lie empty, open, choiceless as a beach – waiting for a gift from the sea.

Anne Morrow Lindbergh, 1906–2001
American aviator, writer

$\mathcal{L}$ike the bee

gathering honey from different flowers,

the wise man

accepts the essence of different scriptures

and sees only the good

in all religions.

Hindu wisdom

We must not,

in trying to think about

how we can make a big difference,

ignore the small daily differences we can make which,

over time, add up to big differences

that we often cannot foresee.

Marian Wright Edelman, b. 1939
American civil rights campaigner

*I*t is good to dream,

but it is better to dream and work.

Faith is mighty,

but action with faith is mightier.

Desiring is helpful,

but work and desire are invincible.

Thomas Robert Gaines
American author

*M*an is

what he believes.

Anton Chekhov, 1860–1904
Russian dramatist

$\mathcal{U}$se your gifts faithfully,

and they shall be enlarged;

practice what you know,

and you shall attain

to higher knowledge.

Matthew Arnold, 1822–1888
English poet, critic, essayist

*E*nthusiasm

is nothing more or less

than faith in action.

Henry Chester, 1858–1879
English clergyman

*T*ouched by grace,

highly unlikely beneficial events

happen to us all the time,

quietly, knocking on the door of our awareness

no more dramatically than the beetle

gently tapping on the windowpane.

M. Scott Peck, b. 1936
American psychiatrist, writer

*T*he mason asks but a narrow shelf

to spring his brick from;

man requires only an infinitely narrower one

to spring his arch of faith from.

Henry David Thoreau, 1817–1862
American essayist, social critic, writer

*H*e who loses money, loses much;

He who loses a friend, loses much more;

He who loses faith, loses all.

Eleanor Roosevelt, 1884–1962
First Lady of the United States of America

$\mathcal{D}$on't waste life in doubts and fears;

spend yourself on the work before you,

well assured that the right performance

of this hour's duties will be the best preparation

for the hours and ages that will follow it.

Ralph Waldo Emerson, 1803–1882
American essayist, philosopher

A man of courage

is also full of faith.

Cicero, 106–43 BC
Roman orator, statesman, essayist

*W*e have just enough religion
to make us hate but not enough
to make us love one another.

Jonathan Swift, 1667–1745
Irish satirist, poet, essayist, cleric

Life

is the childhood

of our immortality.

Johann Wolfgang von Goethe, 1749–1832
German poet, writer, dramatist, scientist

We cannot describe

the natural history of the soul,

but we know that it is divine.

Ralph Waldo Emerson, 1803–1882
American writer, philosopher

The body of a man

is not a home but an inn –

and that only briefly.

Seneca, c. 4 BC–65 AD
Roman philosopher, poet, dramatist, statesman

The true meaning of religion

is thus not simply morality,

but morality touched by emotion.

Mathew Arnold, 1822–1888
English poet, critic, essayist

If I err in the belief

that the souls of men are immortal,

I err gladly,

and I do not wish to lose

so delightful an error.

Cicero, 106–43 BC
Roman orator, statesman, essayist

The whole of mankind

belongs to one religion,

the religion of man.

For all men,

God is the Father.

As the children of one God,

all men are brothers.

Sai Baba
Indian spiritual leader

*I*n life,

every great enterprise begins with

and takes its first forward step

in faith.

Friedrich von Schlegel, 1772–1829
German poet

*E*very tomorrow has two handles.

We can take hold of it

with the handle of anxiety

or the handle of faith.

Henry Ward Beecher, 1813–1887
American clergyman, editor, writer

Life without faith is an arid business.

Noel Coward, 1899–1973
English dramatist, actor, composer

$\mathcal{T}$he ultimate measure of a man

is not where he stands

in moments of comfort and convenience,

but where he stands at times of challenge

and controversy.

Martin Luther King, Jr., 1929–1968
American civil rights leader, minister

*M*y belief certainly seems to get stronger

in the presence of people whose goodness

seems of almost supernatural origin.

Graham Greene, 1904–1991
English writer

Therefore, we are saved by love.

No virtuous act is quite as virtuous from the standpoint

of our friend or foe as from our own;

Therefore, we are saved by the final form of love,

which is forgiveness.

Martin Luther King, Jr., 1929–1968
American civil rights leader, minister

*N*othing worth doing is completed in our lifetime,

Therefore, we are saved by hope.

Nothing true or beautiful or good makes complete

      sense in any immediate context of history;

Therefore, we are saved by faith.

Nothing we do, however virtuous, can be

      accomplished alone.

There are many things that are essential

to arriving at true peace of mind,

and one of the most important is faith,

which cannot be acquired without prayer.

Dwight Lyman Moody, 1837–1899
American preacher

*T*he guardian angels of life

sometimes fly so high

as to be beyond our sight,

but they are always

looking down upon us.

Jean Paul Richter, 1763–1825
German writer

*W*hatever your heart clings to and
confides in — that is really your God.

Martin Luther, 1483–1546
German theologian

The aloneness of the journey of spiritual growth

is a great burden.

But in the communion of growing consciousness,

of knowing with God,

there is enough joy to sustain us.

M. Scott Peck, b. 1936
American psychiatrist, writer

$\mathcal{S}$piritual progress is like detoxification.

Things have to come up in order to be released.

Once we have healed, then our unhealed places

are forced to the surface.

Marianne Williamson
American author, lecturer

I never knew how to worship
until I knew how to love.

Henry Ward Beecher, 1813–1887
American clergyman, editor, writer

$\mathcal{G}$race is available to everyone.

We are all cloaked in the love of God,

no one less nobly than another.

M. Scott Peck, b. 1936
American psychiatrist, writer

It is wonderful how much time

good people spend fighting the devil.

If they would only expend the same amount of energy

on loving their fellow men,

the devil would die of ennui in his own tracks.

Helen Keller, 1880–1968
American writer, lecturer

Words of Wisdom

$\mathcal{L}$et there be many windows in your soul,

That all the glories of the universe

May beautify it.

Ralph Waldo Trine, 1866–1958
American poet, writer

O Divine Master, grant that I may not so much seek

To be consoled as to console;

To be understood, as to understand;

To be loved, as to love;

For it is in giving that we receive;

It is in pardoning that we are pardoned;

And it is in dying that we are born to Eternal Life.

St. Francis of Assisi, 1181–1226
Founder of the Franciscan Order

*L*ord make me an instrument of Thy peace.

Where there is hatred, let me sow love.

Where there is injury, pardon.

Where there is doubt, faith.

Where there is despair, hope.

Where there is darkness, light.

Where there is sadness, joy.

O God,

help us not to despise or oppose

what we do not understand.

William Penn, 1644–1718
English-born Quaker, founder of Pennsylvania

$\mathcal{H}$ave courage for the greatest sorrows of life

and patience for the small ones,

and when you have accomplished your daily task,

go to sleep in peace.

God is awake.

Victor Hugo, 1802–1885
French poet, writer

*L*et nothing disturb you.

Let nothing frighten you.

Everything passes away except God.

St. Theresa, 1515–1582
Spanish nun

O *Thou who art at home*

Deep in my heart,

Enable me to join You

Deep in my heart.

The Talmud

Oh Lord,

help me to be calm when things go wrong,

to persevere when things are difficult,

to be helpful to those in need,

and to be sympathetic to those

whose hearts are heavy.

Unknown

I thank Thee, Lord,

for knowing me better than I know myself

and for letting me know myself

better than others know me.

I pray Thee then,

make me better than they suppose,

and forgive me for what they do not know.

Abu Bekr, 573–634
Father-in-law of Mohammed, his follower and successor

Oh God,

Grant me the serenity to accept

the things that I cannot change,

the courage to change the things that I can,

and the wisdom to distinguish

the one from the other.

Reinhold Niebuhr, 1892–1971
American theologian

$\mathcal{L}$et me lie down like a stone, O Lord,

and rise up like new bread.

Leo Tolstoy, 1828–1910
Russian writer

Teach me to feel another's Woe,

To hide the Fault I see;

That Mercy I to others show,

That Mercy show to me.

Alexander Pope, 1688–1744
English poet

A single grateful thought

raised to heaven

is the most perfect prayer.

Gotthold Ephraim Lessing, 1729–1781
German writer, philosopher

Be merciful to me, O God ....

In the shadow of Your wings, I find protection

until the raging storms are over.

Psalm 57:1

$\mathcal{L}$ord,

teach me to have faith in Your ways,

to trust in Your love even when

I don't understand Your reasons at times.

Unknown

Prayer is the song of the heart.

It reaches the ear of God even if it is

mingled with the cry and the tumult

of a thousand men.

Kahlil Gibran, 1883–1931
Lebanese poet, artist, mystic

*I*n Prayer, the Lips ne'r act the winning part

Without the sweet concurrence of the Heart.

Robert Herrick, 1591–1674
English poet

*T*hose who mumble do not pray.

Prayers grow like windless trees from silence.

Geoffrey Dutton, 1922–1998
Australian poet

*T*he prayer

that reforms the sinner and heals the sick

is an absolute faith that all things

are possible to God.

Mary Baker Eddy, 1821–1910
American religious leader, writer

Prayer makes the Christian's armor bright;

And Satan trembles when he sees

The weakest saint upon his knees.

William Cowper, 1731–1800
English poet

He prayeth best who loveth best

All things both great and small;

For the dear God who loveth us,

He made and loveth all.

Samuel Taylor Coleridge, 1772–1834
English poet

$\mathcal{M}$ight I behold thee,

Might I know thee,

Might I consider thee,

Might I understand thee,

O Lord of the universe.

Native American tradition

God answers sharp and sudden on some prayers

And thrusts the thing we have prayed for in our face,

A gauntlet with a gift in't.

Elizabeth Barrett Browning, 1806–1861
English poet

O Lord!

Thou knowest how busy I must be this day;

if I forget Thee,

do not Thou forget me.

Sir Jacob Astley, 1579–1652
English commander

$\mathcal{P}$raying is not about asking;

it's about listening ....

It is just opening your eyes

to see what was there all along.

Chagdud Tulku Rinpoche, 1930–2002
Tibetan teacher

I do not pray for success.

I ask for faithfulness.

Mother Teresa of Calcutta, 1910–1997
Albanian-born missionary

Prayer does not change God,

but it changes him who prays.

Soren Kierkegaard, 1813–1855
Danish philosopher

The Power of Prayer

$\mathcal{S}$ilence is a friend

who will never betray.

Confucius, c. 550–478 BC
Chinese philosopher

Settle yourself in solitude,

and you will come upon Him

in yourself.

St. Teresa, 1515–1582
Spanish saint

The more powerful and original

a mind, the more it will incline

to the religion of solitude.

Aldous Huxley, 1894–1963
English writer

$\mathcal{L}$et us then labor for an inward stillness,

An inward stillness and an inward healing,

That perfect silence where the lips and heart are still,

And we no longer entertain

Our own imperfect thought and vain opinions,

But God above speaks in us,

And we wait in singleness of heart

That we may know His will ....

Henry Wadsworth Longfellow, 1807–1882
American poet

In all of us there is

an inner consciousness that tells of God,

an inner voice that speaks to our hearts.

It is a voice that speaks to us intimately, personally,

in a time of quiet meditation.

It is like a lamp unto our feet

and a light unto our path.

---

from AA Program

*I*t is not necessary

to go off on a tour of great cathedrals

in order to find the Deity.

Look within.

You have to sit still to do it.

Albert Schweitzer, 1875–1965
German physician, missionary

$\mathcal{L}$isten, my heart, as only saints have listened:

until some enormous call lifted them off the ground;

yet still they knelt, those impossible people,

undistracted by the sound, intent on listening.

Not that you could endure the voice of God,

far from it. But hear what is whispering,

the endless message forming itself from silence.

Rainer Maria Rilke, 1875–1926
Austrian poet

It is only in solitude, when it has broken

that thick crust of shame that separates us

from one another and separates us all from God,

that we have no secrets from God;

only in solitude do we raise our hearts

to see the Heart of the Universe; only in solitude

does the redeeming hymn of supreme confession

issue from our soul.

Miguel de Unamuno, 1864–1936
Spanish philosopher, poet, writer

There is hardly ever a complete silence in our soul.

God is whispering to us wellnigh incessantly.

Whenever the sounds of the world die out in the soul,

or sink low, then we hear these whisperings of God.

He is always whispering to us,

only we do not always hear because of the noise,

hurry, and distraction which life causes

as it rushes on.

Frederick W. Faber, 1814–1863
British rector

Whoso, therefore, withdraweth himself

from his acquaintances and friends,

God will draw near unto him

with His holy angels.

Thomas à Kempis, 1379–1471
Augustinian monk

$\mathcal{L}$earn to get in touch with the silence within yourself

and know that everything in this life has a purpose.

There are no mistakes, no coincidences;

all events are blessings given to us to learn from.

Elisabeth Kübler-Ross, 1926–2004
Swiss-born American psychiatrist, writer

*I*f you wish to grow in your spiritual life,

you must not allow yourself to be caught up

in the workings of the world;

you must find time alone

away from the noise and confusion,

away from the allure of power and wealth.

Thomas à Kempis, 1379–1471
Augustinian monk

*T*he highest of all human experiences

will be ours when we retire

into the Great Empire of Silence

and meet with the Eternal Spirit.

Robert Merrill Bartlett, 1888–1995
British theologian

*S*olitude is when you discover

God firsthand.

You don't need an intermediary.

Buckminster Fuller, 1895–1983
American architect, philosopher

The more faithfully you listen

to the voice within you,

the better you will hear

what is sounding outside.

Dag Hammarskjöld, 1905–1961
Swedish UN Secretary-General

$\mathcal{I}$nside myself

is a place where I live all alone,

and that's where you renew your springs

that never dry up.

Pearl. S. Buck, 1892–1973
American writer

We need to find God, and he

cannot be found in noise and restlessness.

God is the friend of silence.

See how nature –

trees, flowers, grass – grow in silence;

see the stars, the moon and sun,

how they move in Silence ….

The more we receive in silent prayer,

the more we can give in our active life.

We need silence to be able to touch souls.

Mother Teresa of Calcutta, 1910–1997
Albanian-born missionary

When you have closed your doors

and darkened your room,

remember never to say that you are alone,

for you are not alone;

God is within, and your genius is within –

and what need have they of light

to see what you are doing?

Epictetus, c. 55–135 BC
Greek philosopher

*I*n the rush and noise of life, as you have intervals,

step home within yourself and be still.

Wait upon God, and feel His good presence;

this will carry you evenly through your day's business.

William Penn, 1644–1718
English-born Quaker, founder of Pennsylvania

When we keep a diagnostic eye on our soul,

then we can become familiar with the different,

often complex, stirrings of our inner life

and travel with confidence on the paths

that lead to the light.

Henri J. M. Nouwen, 1932–1996
Roman Catholic priest

*Genuine tranquility of the heart
and perfect peace of mind,
the highest blessings on earth after health,
are to be found only in solitude and,
as a permanent disposition,
only in the deepest seclusion.*

Arthur Schopenhauer, 1788–1860
German philosopher

Finding God in Silence

I have to live with myself, and so

I want to be fit for myself to know;

I want to be able, as days go by,

Always to look myself straight in the eye.

Edgar A. Guest, 1881–1959
English-born American poet, author

*I*n matters of style,

swim with the current;

in matters of principle,

stand like a rock.

Thomas Jefferson, 1743–1826
President of the United States of America

*H*ere is a rule to remember in future

when anything tempts you to be bitter:

Don't think, 'This is a misfortune' but,

'To bear this worthily is a good fortune.'

Marcus Aurelius, 121–180 AD
Roman emperor, philosopher

I will try always to recognize and submit to the gods

in me and the gods in other men and women.

There is my creed.

D. H. Lawrence, 1885–1930
English writer, poet

$\mathcal{I}$n spite of everything, I still believe that people are really good at heart. I simply can't build up my hopes on a foundation consisting of confusion, misery, and death.

Anne Frank, 1929–1945
Dutch schoolgirl, diarist

However mean your life is, meet it and live it;

do not shun it and call it hard names.

Cultivate poverty like a garden herb, like sage.

Do not trouble yourself much to get new things,

whether clothes or friends.

Things do not change; we change.

Sell your clothes and keep your thoughts.

Henry David Thoreau, 1817–1962
American essayist, social critic, writer

I believe that it is better to tell the truth than a lie. I believe it is better to be free than to be a slave. And I believe it is better to know than to be ignorant.

H. L. Mencken, 1880–1956
American writer, critic, satirist

$\mathcal{S}$ome good must come by clinging to the right.

Conscience is a man's compass, and though the needle

sometimes deviates, though one perceives irregularities

in directing one's course by it, still one must try

to follow its direction.

Vincent Van Gough, 1853–1890
Dutch post-impressionist painter

$\mathcal{I}$ wanted to avoid violence.

Non-violence is the first article of my faith.

It is also the last article of my creed.

Mahatma Gandhi, 1869–1948
Indian political leader

$\mathcal{T}$his I do believe above all,

especially in my times of greater discouragement,

that I must believe – that I must believe

in my fellow men – that I must believe in myself –

and I must believe in God – if life

is to have any meaning.

Margaret Chase Smith, 1897–1995
American senator

I desire so to conduct the affairs
of this administration that if at the end,
when I come to lay down the reins of power,
I have lost every other friend on earth,
I shall at least have one friend left,
and that friend shall be down inside me.

Abraham Lincoln, 1809–1865
President of the United States of America

It makes all the difference in the world to your life

whether you arrive at a philosophy and a religion or not.

It makes the difference between living in a world

which is a constantly changing mass of phenomena

and living in a significant, ordered universe.

Mary Ellen Chase, 1887–1973
American educator, author

_D_o whatever comes your way … as well as you can.

Think as little as possible about yourself.

Think as much as possible about other people ….

Since you get more joy out of giving to others,

you should put a good deal more thought into

the happiness that you are able to give.

Eleanor Roosevelt, 1884–1962
First Lady of the United States of America

*S*o many gods, so many creeds,

So many paths that wind and wind,

While just the art of being kind

Is all the sad world needs.

Ella Wheeler Wilcox, 1850–1919
American writer, poet

These, then, are my last words to you:

Be not afraid of life.

Believe that life is worth living,

and your belief will help create that fact.

William James, 1842–1910
American psychologist, philosopher

$\mathcal{T}$his I believe:

that the free, exploring mind of the individual

human is the most valuable thing in the world.

And this I would fight for:

the freedom of the mind to take any direction

it wishes, undirected.

And this I must fight against:

any idea, religion, or government which limits

or destroys the individual.

John Steinbeck, 1902–1968
American writer

$\mathcal{L}$ove the earth and sun and the animals;

despise riches; give alms to everyone that asks;

stand up for the stupid and crazy;

devote your income and labor to others;

hate tyrants; argue not concerning God;

have patience and indulgence toward the people;

take off your hat to nothing known or unknown

or to any man ....

Walt Whitman, 1819–1892
American poet, writer

There's harmony and inner peace

to be found in following a moral compass

that points in the same direction

regardless of fashion or trend.

Ted Koppel, b. 1940
American TV anchor

*M*y country is the world,

and my religion is to do good.

Thomas Paine, 1737–1809
American political theorist

Be a good human being,

a warm-hearted, affectionate person.

That is my fundamental belief.

Having a sense of caring, a feeling of compassion,

will bring happiness or peace of mind to oneself

and automatically create a positive attitude.

Dalai Lama, b.1935
Tibetan spiritual leader

I never submitted

the whole system of my opinions to the

creed of any party of men whatever, in religion,

in philosophy, in politics or in anything else,

where I was capable of thinking for myself.

Such an addiction is the last degradation

of a free and moral agent.

If I could not go to Heaven but with a party,

I would not go there at all.

Thomas Jefferson, 1743–1826
President of the United States of America

I have one life and one chance
to make it count for something …. I'm free to choose
what that something is, and the something I've chosen
is my faith. Now, my faith goes beyond theology and
religion and requires considerable work and effort.
My faith demands … that I do whatever I can,
wherever I am, whenever I can, for as long as I can
with whatever I have to try to make a difference.

Jimmy Carter, b. 1924
President of the United States of America

Hold faithfulness and sincerity

as first principles.

Confucius, c. 550–478 BC
Chinese philosopher

Personal Creeds

A faith

which does not doubt

is a dead faith.

Miguel de Unamuno, 1864–1936
Spanish philosopher, poet, writer

*T*here lives more faith in honest doubt,

Believe me, than in half the creeds.

Lord Alfred Tennyson, 1809–1892
English poet

*I*n faith, there is enough light

for those who want to believe

and enough shadow

to blind those who don't.

Blaise Pascal, 1623–1662
French mathematician

$\mathcal{G}$od does not die on the day

we cease to believe in a personal deity,

but we die on the day when our lives

cease to be illumined by the steady radiance,

renewed daily, of a wonder, the source of which

is beyond all reason.

Dag Hammarskjöld, 1905–1961
Swedish UN Secretary-General

$\mathcal{T}$o deny, to believe,

and to doubt absolutely –

this is for man what

running is for a horse.

Blaise Pascal, 1623–1662
French mathematician

$\mathcal{Y}$es, I have doubted.

I have wandered off the path.

I have been lost.

But I always returned.

It is beyond the logic I seek.

It is intuitive – an intrinsic,

built-in sense of direction.

I seem to find my way home.

My faith has wavered but has saved me.

Helen Hayes, 1900–1993
American actress

When men destroy their old gods

they will find new ones

to take their place.

Pearl S. Buck, 1892–1973
American writer

*O*ne by one, like leaves from a tree,

All my faiths have forsaken me.

Sara Teasdale, 1884–1933
American poet

$\mathcal{D}$oubt is part of all religions.

All the religious thinkers were doubters.

Isaac Bashevis Singer, 1902–1991
Polish-born Jewish writer

A faith that cannot survive

collision with the truth

is not worth many regrets.

Arthur C. Clarke, b. 1917
English novelist

$\mathcal{S}$ometimes God lets you and me struggle

until we recognize our dependence on Him.

In so doing,

He gives our faith an opportunity

to grow and mature.

James Dobson, b. 1936
American psychologist

If I lose my direction,

I have to look for the North Star,

and I go to the north.

That does not mean

I expect to arrive at the North Star;

I just want to go in that direction.

Thich Nhat Hanh, b. 1926
Vietnamese Buddhist monk

Faith and doubt both are needed —

not as antagonists but working side by side

to take us around the unknown curve.

Lillian Smith, 1897–1966
American social activist

To have doubted

one's own first principles

is the mark of a civilized man.

Oliver Wendell Holmes, Jr., 1841–1935
American judge, jurist

If you have abandoned one faith,

do not abandon all faith.

There is always an alternative

to the faith we lose.

Or is it the same faith

under another mask?

Graham Greene, 1904–1991
English writer

*T*here seems to be a terrible misunderstanding

on the part of a great many people

to the effect that when you cease to believe

you may cease to behave.

Louis Kronenberger, 1904–1980
American critic

$\mathcal{F}$aith is not a thing

which one loses;

we merely cease

to shape our lives by it.

Georges Bernanos, 1888–1948
French writer

A faith that hasn't been tested can't be trusted.

Adrian Rogers
American preacher

The beginning of wisdom

is found in doubting;

by doubting

we come to the question,

and by seeking

we may come upon the truth.

Pièrre Abelard, 1079–1141
French philosopher

Doubt is a pain

too lonely to know that

faith is his twin brother.

Kahlil Gibran, 1883–1931
Lebanese poet, artist, mystic

*W*hen walking through
the 'valley of shadows' remember,
a shadow is cast
by a light.

Unknown

Faith and Doubt

If you desire faith,

then you have faith enough.

Elizabeth Barrett Browning, 1806–1861
English poet

*Not Truth, but Faith it is
that keeps the world alive.*

Edna St. Vincent Millay, 1892–1950
American poet, author

Going to heaven! …

How dim it sounds!

And yet it will be done

As sure as flocks go home at night

Unto the shepherd's arm!

Emily Dickinson, 1830–1886
American poet

*R*eason is our soul's left hand,

Faith her right.

John Donne, 1572–1631
English poet

*B*ut I float on the bosom of faith

that bears me along like a river;

And the lamp of my soul

is alight with love for life

and the world and the Giver.

Ella Wheeler Wilcox, 1850–1919
American writer, poet

I know not where his islands lift

Their fronded palms in air.

I only know I cannot drift

Beyond his love and care.

John Greenleaf Whittier, 1807–1892
American poet

Here in the maddening maze of things,

When tossed by storm or flood,

To one fixed ground, my spirit clings;

I know that God is good.

I know not what the future hath,

Of marvel or surprise,

Assured alone that life and death

His mercy underlies.

Oh may I join the choir invisible

Of those immortal dead who live again

In minds made better by their presence.

George Eliot, 1819–1880
English writer, poet

The One remains;

The many change and pass;

Heaven's light forever shines.

Percy Bysshe Shelley, 1792–1822
English poet, dramatist, essayist

To see a World in a grain of Sand

And a heaven in a Wild Flower,

Hold Infinity in the palm of your hand

And Eternity in an hour.

William Blake, 1757–1827
English poet

$\mathcal{P}$ray for my soul.

More things are wrought by prayer

Than this world dreams of.

Lord Alfred Tennyson, 1809–1892
English poet

Give me my scallop-shell of quiet,

My staff of faith to walk upon,

My scrip of joy, immortal diet,

My bottle of salvation,

My gown of glory, hope's true gage;

And thus I'll take my pilgrimage.

Sir Walter Raleigh, 1554–1618
English courtier, explorer, poet, essayist

*O*ur birth is but a sleep and a forgetting;

   The soul that rises with us, our life's star,

Hath had elsewhere its setting,

   And cometh from afar:

Not in entire forgetfulness,

And not in utter nakedness,

But trailing clouds of glory do we come

   From God, who is our home.

William Wordsworth, 1770–1850
English poet

$\mathscr{F}$or nothing worth proving can be proven,

Nor yet disproven: Wherefore thou be wise,

Cleave ever to the sunnier side of doubt.

Lord Alfred Tennyson, 1809–1892
English poet

No coward soul is mine,

No trembler in the world's storm-troubled sphere:

I see Heaven's glories shine,

And faith shines equal, arming me from fear.

Emily Brontë, 1818–1848
English poet, writer

*T*here is no unbelief;

Whoever plants a seed beneath the sod

And waits to see it push away the clod,

He trusts in God.

Elizabeth York Case, 1840–1911
American writer, poet

God be prais'd, that to believing souls

Gives light in darkness, comfort in despair.

William Shakespeare, 1564–1616
English poet, dramatist

$\mathscr{F}$aith is the subtle chain

Which binds us to the infinite; the voice

Of deep life within, that will remain

Until we crowd it hence.

Elizabeth Oakes Smith, 1806–1893
American poet, writer

If faith produce no works, I see

That faith is not a living tree.

Hannah More, 1745–1833
British writer, social reformer

To us also, through every star,

through every blade of grass,

is not God made visible if we will

open our minds and our eyes?

Thomas Carlyle, 1795–1881
Scottish historian, critic, essayist

$\mathcal{I}$ see something of God

Each hour of the twenty-four,

And each moment then,

In the faces of men and women, I see God,

And in my own face in the glass ….

Walt Whitman, 1819–1892
American poet, writer

Faith builds a bridge across the gulf of Death,

To break the shock blind nature cannot shun,

And lands Thought smoothly on the further shore.

Edward Young, 1683–1765
English poet

I never saw a moor,

I never saw the sea;

Yet know I how the heather looks,

And what a wave must be.

I never spoke with God,

Nor visited in heaven;

Yet certain am I of the spot

As if the chart were given.

Emily Dickinson, 1830–1886
American poet

In the Words of the Poets

*F*aith enables persons to be persons

because it lets God be God.

Carter Lindberg, b. 1937
American professor of theology

$\mathcal{F}$ear can keep us up all night long,

but faith makes one fine pillow.

Unknown

*M*iracles happen to those

who believe in them.

Bernard Berenson, 1865–1959
American art critic

Faith is like electricity.

You can't see it,

but you can see the light.

Unknown

*F*aith is not something to grasp;

it is a state to grow into.

Mahatma Gandhi, 1869–1948
Indian political leader

To one who has faith,

no explanation is necessary.

To one without faith,

no explanation is possible.

St. Thomas Aquinas, 1225–1274
Dominician monk

On a long journey of human life,

faith is the best of companions;

it is the best refreshment on the journey;

and it is the greatest property.

Buddha, c. 560–480 BC
Indian spiritual leader, founder of Buddhism

$\mathcal{F}$aith moves mountains,

but you have to keep pushing

while you are praying.

Mason Cooley, b. 1927
American aphorist

Faith is not belief without proof

but trust without reservation.

Elton Trueblood, 1900–1994
American writer, philosopher

With faith,

man can achieve anything.

Faith is the foundation

for the realization of God.

Sai Baba
Indian spiritual leader

$\mathcal{T}$ake the first step in faith.

You don't have to see the whole staircase;

just take the first step.

Martin Luther King Jr., 1929–1968
American civil rights leader, minister

$\mathcal{G}$od cannot be grasped by the mind.

If He could be grasped,

He would not be God.

Evagrius of Pontus, 345–399 AD
Greek theologian

No faith is our own

that we have not

arduously won.

Havelock Ellis, 1859–1939
English doctor, essayist

*T*he world was never conquered by intrigue;

it was conquered by faith.

Benjamin Disraeli, 1804–1881
English statesman, writer

*Y*our faith

is what you believe

not what you know.

John Lancaster Spalding, 1840–1960
American pastor

Faith is different from proof;

the latter is human,

the former is a gift from God.

Blaise Pascal, 1623–1662
French philosopher, physicist

*F*aith is not, contrary to the usual ideas,

something that turns out to be right or wrong,

like a gambler's bet: It's an act, an intention, a project,

something that makes you, in leaping into the future,

go so far, far, far ahead that you shoot clean out of time

and right into Eternity, which is not the end of time or

a whole lot of time or unending time but timelessness,

the old Eternal now.

Joanna Russ, b. 1937
American writer

*F*orgiving means to pardon the unpardonable,

Faith means believing the unbelievable,

And hoping means to hope when things are hopeless.

G.K Chesterton, 1874–1936
English writer, poet, critic

$\mathcal{L}$et faith be thy staff.

Sri Guru Nanak, 1469–1539
Indian founder of Sikhism

A garden is evidence of faith.

It links us with all the misty figures of the past

who also planted and were nourished

by the fruits of their planting.

Gladys Taber, 1899–1980
American teacher, writer

*F*aith is the very first thing
you should pack in a hope chest.

Sarah Ban Breathnach
American writer

$\mathcal{B}$e faithful in small things

because it is in them

that your strength lies.

Mother Teresa of Calcutta, 1910–1997
Albanian-born missionary

We do not believe in immortality

because we can prove it,

but we try to prove it because we

cannot help believing it.

Harriet Martineau, 1802–1876
English writer

$\mathcal{A}$ Christian who looks gloomy

at the mention of death, still more,

one who talks of his friends as if he had lost them,

turns the bushel of his little-faith

over the lamp of the Lord's light.

George MacDonald, 1824–1905
Scottish writer, poet, preacher

$\mathcal{F}$aith is a passionate intuition.

William Wordsworth, 1770–1850
English poet

$\mathcal{F}$aith means living with uncertainty –

feeling your way through life,

letting your heart guide you

like a lantern in the dark.

<hr>

Dan Millman
American world champion athlete, professor, writer

*I*f a man wishes to be sure

of the road he treads on,

he must close his eyes

and walk in the dark.

St. John of the Cross, 1542–1591
Spanish Carmelite monk

*Faith is the strength
by which a shattered world
shall emerge into the light.*

Helen Keller, 1880–1968
American writer, lecturer

$\mathcal{F}$aith is not an easy virtue,

but in the broad world of man's total voyage

through time to eternity,

faith is not only a gracious companion

but an essential guide.

Theodore M. Hesburgh, b. 1917
American clergyman

$\mathscr{T}$here is nothing that wastes the body like worry,

and one who has any faith in God should be ashamed

to worry about anything whatsoever.

Mahatma Gandhi, 1869–1948
Indian political leader

$\mathcal{F}$aith is the highest passion

in a human being.

Many in every generation

may not come that far,

but none comes further.

Soren Kierkegaard, 1813–1855
Danish philosopher, theologian

*O*nly faith in a life after death,

in a brighter world where dear ones will meet again –

only that and the measured tramp of time –

can give consolation.

Sir Winston Churchill, 1874–1965
British Prime Minister, statesman, writer

Faith is an excitement and an enthusiasm;

it is a condition of intellectual magnificence

to which we must cling as to a treasure

and not squander in …

priggish argument.

George Sand, 1804–1876
French writer, dramatist

*N*othing in this world is so marvelous
as the transformation that a soul undergoes
when the light of faith descends
upon the light of reason.

W. Bernard Ullathorne
English writer

$\mathcal{F}$aith is,

at one and the same time,

absolutely necessary

and altogether

impossible.

Stanislaw Lem, b. 1921
Polish writer

The reason why birds can fly and we can't

is simply that they have perfect faith,

for to have faith is to have wings.

J. M. Barrie, 1860–1937
Scottish writer, dramatist

$\mathcal{A}$ little faith will bring your soul to heaven;

a great faith will bring heaven to your soul.

Charles Spurgeon, 1834–1892
British preacher

$\mathscr{A}$s your faith strengthens,

you will find that there is no longer the need

to have a sense of control,

that things will flow as they will,

and that you will flow with them

to your great delight and benefit.

Emmanuel Teney
American professor of psychiatry

Faith is an oasis in the heart

which will never be reached

by the caravan of thinking.

Kahlil Gibran, 1883–1931
Lebanese poet, artist, mystic

$\mathcal{S}$cientists were rated as great heretics by the church,

but they were truly religious men because of

their faith in the orderliness of the universe.

Albert Einstein, 1879–1955
German-born American physicist

*W*ithout faith, nothing is possible.

With it, nothing is impossible.

Mary McLeod Bethune, 1875–1955
American educator

*F*aith is believing when it is

beyond the power of reason

to believe.

Voltaire, 1694–1778
French philosopher, dramatist, poet, writer

$\mathcal{R}$eason itself is a matter of faith.

It is an act of faith

to assert that our thoughts

have any relation to reality.

G. K. Chesterton, 1874–1936
English writer, poet, critic

Faith is to believe

what you do not see;

the reward of this faith

is to see what you believe.

St. Augustine, 354–430 BC
Christian theologian, philosopher

*G*od has made many doors

opening into truth which

He opens to all who knock upon them

with the hands of faith.

Kahlil Gibran, 1883–1931
Lebanese poet, artist, mystic

$\mathcal{T}$he way to see by faith

is to shut the eye of reason.

Benjamin Franklin, 1706–1790
American inventor

$\mathcal{H}$e who has faith has …

an inward reservoir of courage, hope,

confidence, calmness, and assuring trust

that all will come out well –

even though to the world

it may appear to come out badly.

B.C. Forbes, 1880–1954
Scottish-born American financial journalist

The bread of life is love;

the salt of love is work;

the sweetness of life is poetry;

and the water of life is faith.

Anna Jameson, 1794–1860
English writer

Faith is like the bird

that feels the light

when the dawn is still dark.

Rabindranath Tagore, 1861–1941
Bengali poet, philosopher

*F*aith is not a delicate flower, which would

wither under the slightest stormy weather.

Faith is like the Himalayan Mountains,

which cannot possibly change.

No storm can possibly remove

the Himalayan Mountains

from their foundations.

Mahatma Gandhi, 1869–1948
Indian political leader

The smallest seed of faith

is better than

the largest fruit of happiness.

Henry David Thoreau, 1817–1862
American essayist, social critic, writer

Reflections on Faith

$\mathcal{L}$et us raise a standard

to which the wise and honest can repair;

the rest is in the hands of God.

George Washington, 1732–1799
President of the United States of America

I am positive I have a soul:

nor can all the books

with which the materialists have

pestered the world ever convince me

of the contrary.

Laurence Sterne, 1713–1768
Irish-born English writer, clergyman

*I*n the midst of dangers,

I have felt an inner calm

and known resources of strength

that only God could give.

In many instances,

I have felt the power of God

transforming the fatigue of despair

into the buoyancy of hope.

Martin Luther King, Jr., 1929–1968
American civil rights leader, minister

I pray hard,

work hard,

and leave the rest to God.

Florence Griffith Joyner, b. 1953
American track athlete

*F*aith is a living,

daring confidence in God's grace,

so sure and certain that a man

could stake his life on it

a thousand times.

Martin Luther, 1483–1546
German theologian

I believe in God

and in nature

and in the triumph

of good over evil.

Johann Wolfgang von Goethe, 1749–1832
German poet, writer, dramatist, scientist

$\mathcal{I}$ am convinced that the universe
is under the control of a loving purpose
and that in the struggle for righteousness
man has cosmic companionship.
Behind the harsh appearances of the world
is a benign power.

Martin Luther King, Jr., 1929–1968
American civil rights leader, minister

We know that the soul survives the body
and that, being set free from the bars of the body,
it sees with clear gaze those things which before,
dwelling in the body, it could not see.

St. Ambrose, c. 340–397
Bishop of Milan

*N*ature had created us

with the capacity to know God,

to experience God.

Alice Walker, b. 1944
American author

I believe God is in me

as the sun is in the color

and fragrance of a flower –

the light in my darkness,

the voice in my silence.

Helen Keller, 1880–1968
American writer, lecturer

I believe in

God the Father Almighty

because wherever I have looked,

through all that I see around me,

I see the trace of an intelligent mind,

and because in natural laws,

and especially in the laws which govern

the social relations of men,

I see not merely the proofs of an intelligence

but the proofs of beneficence.

Henry George, 1839–1897
American economist

$\mathcal{T}$he believer acquaints himself

with the sacred realities

through deep senses

different from those used by others ....

The believer lives

for all the days and the nights,

and the unfaithful live

but a few hours.

Kahlil Gibran, 1883–1931
Lebanese poet, artist, mystic

$\mathcal{T}$he only limit

to our realization of tomorrow

will be our doubts of today.

Let us move forward

with strong and active faith.

Franklin D. Roosevelt, 1882–1945
President of the United States of America

$\mathcal{T}$en thousand difficulties
do not make one doubt.

John Newman, 1801–1890
English Cardinal, theologian, poet

I know God will not give me

anything I can't handle.

I just wish that he

didn't trust me so much.

Mother Teresa of Calcutta, 1910–1997
Albanian-born missionary

The ablest men in all walks of modern life

are men of faith.

Most of them have much more faith

than they themselves realize.

Bruce Barton, 1886–1967
American advertising executive

$\mathcal{T}$he suffering and agonizing moments

through which I have passed over the last few years

have also drawn me closer to God.

More than ever before I am convinced

of the reality of a personal God.

Martin Luther King, Jr., 1929–1968
American civil rights leader, minister

Men and Women of Faith

this anthology will provide you with ideas to contemplate, words to sooth, and questions to consider as you continue on your journey.

PREFACE

From Buddha to St. Teresa to Einstein, the authors, poets, and world leaders represented in this inspirational anthology state their spiritual reflections from the perspective of many different faiths and creeds. Not surprisingly, among the most beautiful reflections are those written by renowned poets, such as Wordsworth, Blake, and Whitman. You will also find the poignant words of that great man of faith, civil rights leader and minister, Martin Luther King, Jr., who wrote movingly of the strength he drew from his unwavering belief in God during the bitter conflicts he faced.

These words of faith also speak to the inevitable existence of doubt, the necessity for solitude, and the essence of God no matter the religion or creed to which one adheres. Through these reflections, it becomes clear that faith is a personal, intuitive state of mind that takes many differing forms. No matter where you are in your faith—whether religious, spiritual, or intellectual—

CONTENTS

Preface

Men and Women of Faith

Reflections on Faith

In the Words of the Poets

Faith and Doubt

Personal Creeds

Finding God in Silence

The Power of Prayer

Words of Wisdom

Anthology: Margaret Miller
Design: Zoë Murphy

This anthology © The Five Mile Press Pty Ltd

This edition published in the United States in 2006 by School Specialty
Publishing, a member of the School Specialty Family.

Library of Congress Cataloging-in-Publication Data is on file with the publisher.

Send all inquiries to:

School Specialty Publishing
8720 Orion Place
Colombus, OH 43240-2111

ISBN 0-7696-4715-4

Printed in China
1 2 3 4 5 6 7 8 9 FMP 09 08 07 06 05

www.SchoolSpecialtyPublishing.com

Enduring Words

OF

FAITH

Enduring Words

OF

FAITH